Stay Healthy!

Why do we need to be active?

Angela Royston

www.raintreepublishers.co.uk
Visit our website to find out more information about **Raintree** books.

To order:
 Phone 44 (0) 1865 888112
 Send a fax to 44 (0) 1865 314091
 Visit the Raintree Bookshop at **www.raintreepublishers.co.uk** to browse our catalogue and order online.

First published in Great Britain by Raintree, Halley Court, Jordan Hill, Oxford OX2 8EJ, part of Harcourt Education.
Raintree is a registered trademark of Harcourt Education Ltd.

© Harcourt Education Ltd 2006
First printed in paperback in 2007.
The moral right of the proprietor has been asserted.

Editorial: Jilly Attwood
Design: Jo Hinton-Malivoire, bigtop
Picture Research: Ruth Blair, Ginny Stroud-Lewis
Production: Severine Ribierre
Originated by Modern Age
Printed and bound in China by South China Printing Company

10 digit ISBN 1 406 20048 4 (hardback)
13 digit ISBN 978 1 406 20048 5 (hardback)
10 09 08 07 06
10 9 8 7 6 5 4 3 2 1
10 digit ISBN 1 406 20053 0 (paperback)
13 digit ISBN 978 1 406 20053 9 (paperback)
11 10 09 08
10 9 8 7 6 5 4 3 2

British Library Cataloguing in Publication Data
Royston, Angela
Why do we need to be active?. - (Stay healthy!)
613.7
A full catalogue record for this book is available from the British Library.

Acknowledgements
The publishers would like to thank the following for permission to reproduce photographs:
Alamy Images p.5(Geogphotos), p.7(Brand X Pictures), p.16(David Crausby), p.18 & 23d(Stock Image); Corbis pp.4, 11, 13, p.15& 23e(Norbert Schaefer), 21, 23a; Getty Images pp.6, 17& 23b(Photodisc), pp.8, 9, 19(The Image Bank), p.20(Stone), p.22(Digital Vision); Harcourt Education pp.10, 12, 14, 23c(Tudor Photography).

Cover photograph of girls swimming reproduced with permission of Getty Images/Photodisc. Back cover images reproduced with permission of Corbis and Alamy Images (Brand X Pictures).

Every effort has been made to contact copyright holders of any material reproduced in this book. Any omissions will be rectified in subsequent printings if notice is given to the publishers.

Our thanks to Dr Sarah Schenker, Dietitian, for her help in the preparation of this book.

Some words are shown in bold, **like this**. You can find them in the picture glossary on page 23.

Contents

What does being active mean?

When you move you are being active.

Running is being active.

When you **exercise** you are being active.

Climbing stairs is good exercise.

Why do we need to be active?

Being active helps your body to work better.

Swimming **exercises** your arms and legs.

Catching a ball helps your eyes and hands work well together.

What helps you to run fast?

You use your **muscles** to move your body.

Who do you think will win this race?

This boy won!

Practising helps you to run faster.

Why do you puff and pant?

You puff and pant when you are out of breath.

Your body needs more air.

lung

The air goes into your **lungs**.

Does your heart beat faster when you are out of breath?

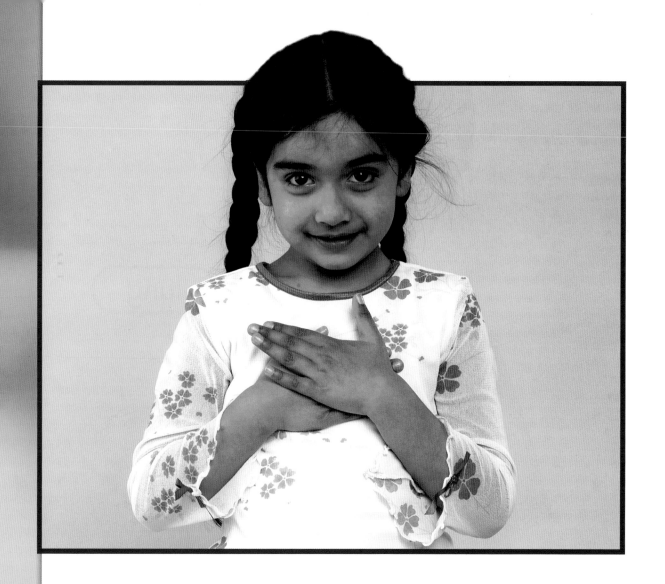

Your heart does beat faster when you are out of breath.

You can feel your heart beating in your chest.

You **exercise** your heart and **lungs** when you are out of breath.

Why does exercise make you hot?

Your **muscles** make heat when they are working hard.

The heat spreads through all your body.

Sweating helps to cool you down.

How does climbing help your body?

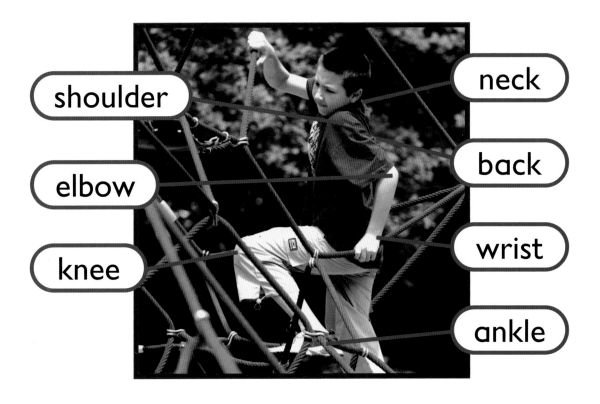

shoulder

neck

elbow

back

knee

wrist

ankle

Climbing **exercises** your **muscles** and **joints**.

This photo shows the main joints.

Which joints do you use to swing?

You use your shoulder joints
to swing.

Which is more active?

Which is more active, riding a bike or pushing a scooter?

Try it!

Which one makes your heart beat faster?

What happens if you are not active?

If you are not active at all, your body gets weaker.

But when you are active you need to rest sometimes.

Why do you need to sleep?

Your body rests when you are asleep.

It gets ready to be active again the next day!

Glossary

 **exercise** using your muscles to move

 **joint** where bones join up, such as in your knee, to let you move and bend

 **lung** part of your body inside your chest that takes in air

 **muscle** fleshy part of your body that helps you to move

 **sweating** losing salty water made by your skin. This helps you to cool down.

Index

Note to parents and teachers

Reading non-fiction texts for information is an important part of a child's literacy development. Readers can be encouraged to ask simple questions and then use the text to find the answers. Most chapters in this book begin with a question. Read the questions together. Look at the pictures. Talk about what the answer might be. Then read the text to find out if your predictions were correct. To develop readers' enquiry skills, encourage them to think of other questions they might ask about the topic. Discuss where you could find the answers. Assist children in using the contents page, picture glossary and index to practise research skills and new vocabulary.